HOLIDAYS AND FESTIVALS

Memorial Day

Rebecca Rissman

Heinemann Library
Chicago, Illinois

www.heinemannraintree.com
Visit our website to find out more information about Heinemann-Raintree books.

To order:

☎ Phone 888-454-2279

⌨ Visit www.heinemannraintree.com to browse our catalog and order online.

Edited by Adrian Vigliano and Rebecca Rissman
Designed by Ryan Frieson
Picture research by Tracy Cummins
Leveling by Nancy E. Harris
Originated by Capstone Global Library Ltd.
Printed in China by South China Printing Company Ltd.

15 14 13 12 11 10
10 9 8 7 6 5 4 3 2 1

Library of Congress Cataloging-in-Publication Data
Rissman, Rebecca.
  Memorial Day / Rebecca Rissman.
    p. cm.—(Holidays and festivals)
  Includes bibliographical references and index.
  ISBN 978-1-4329-4054-6 (hc)—ISBN 978-1-4329-4073-7 (pb) 1.
Memorial Day—Juvenile literature. I. Title.
  E642.R57 2011
  394.262—dc22
                                    2009052854

Acknowledgments

The author and publishers are grateful to the following for permission to reproduce copyright material: AP Photo/Lisa Poole **p.4**; AP Photo/Chris Gardner **p.19**; Corbis ©Michael Reynolds/EPA **p.5**; Corbis ©Jim Young/Reuters **p.15**; Corbis ©Ariel Skelley **p.18**; Corbis ©Jay Syverson **p.21**; Corbis ©Jim Young/Reuters **p.23c**; Getty Images **p.8**; Getty Images/MPI **p.10**; Getty Images/Brendan Smialowski **p.16**; Getty Images/KAREN BLEIER/AFP **p.17**; Getty Images/KAREN BLEIER/AFP **p.23a**; Getty Images **p.23b**; istockphoto ©John Clines **p.22**; Library of Congress Prints and Photographs Division **pp.7, 11, 23d**; National Archive **p.9**; Shutterstock ©Jeremy R. Smith Sr. **p.14**; Shutterstock ©Lee Prince **p.20**; The Granger Collection, New York **pp.6, 12, 13**.

Cover photograph of American flags placed on gravestones in Arlington, VA reproduced with permission of Getty Images/Mark Wilson. Back cover photograph reproduced with permission of Shutterstock ©Jeremy R. Smith Sr.

Every effort has been made to contact copyright holders of any material reproduced in this book. Any omissions will be rectified in subsequent printings if notice is given to the publisher.

Contents

What Is a Holiday?

People celebrate holidays.
A holiday is a special day.

Memorial Day is a holiday.
Memorial Day is in May.

The Story of Memorial Day

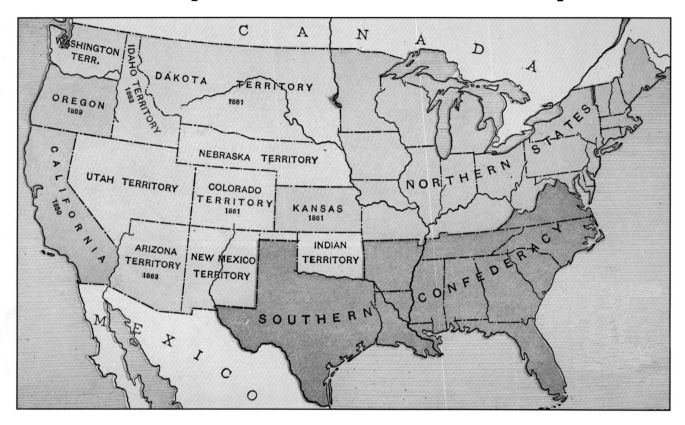

In 1860 two parts of America fought each other. The two parts were the North and the South.

6

This fight was called the Civil War.

The South wanted to become a
new country. The South wanted to
8 have slaves.

The North did not want the South to become a new country. The North wanted to free the slaves.

In 1865 the North won the war. The slaves were free.

Many Americans died in the war.
People in the North and the South
were very sad.

People put flowers on the graves of soldiers from the North and the South.

The people showed that they were thankful for what the soldiers had done.

Celebrating Memorial Day

On Memorial Day people remember soldiers who died fighting for the United States.

People give thanks for soldiers.

People leave flags and flowers
on graves.

People fly the American flag at half-mast to honor soldiers.

People come together to listen to
music and eat food.

People think and talk about the United States.

Memorial Day Symbols

The American flag is a symbol of Memorial Day.

Graves decorated with flowers and flags are symbols of Memorial Day.

Calendar

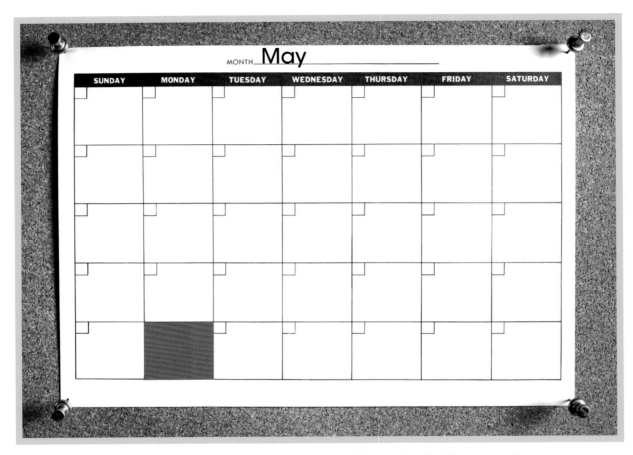

Memorial Day is the last Monday in May.

Picture Glossary

 **half-mast** when flags are flown in the middle of a flagpole

 **slaves** people who are forced to work for no pay

 **soldiers** people who serve in the military

 **war** a fight between two or more countries or groups

Index

Note to Parents and Teachers

Before reading

Briefly explain the armed forces including the five branches. Explain that every May Americans recognize Memorial Day, a special day when we remember those who have lost their lives in war. Some children will have personal experience with family or friends who currently serve in the military or have been killed in battle. For others, death will still be a more abstract concept. Allow the children to talk about these experiences.

After reading

Using art supplies and butcher paper, create a wall of remembrance. Have the children draw pictures and write words of people, pets, or events that have passed that they want to remember. Explain that remembering is another way we "memorialize" something or someone.